Our Senses
Taste

Kay Woodward

HODDER
Wayland

an imprint of Hodder Children's Books

Our Senses
Hearing ● Sight ● Smell ● Taste ● Touch

For more information on this series and other Hodder Wayland titles,
go to www.hodderwayland.co.uk

Senses – Taste

Copyright © 2005 Hodder Wayland
First published in 2005 by Hodder Wayland,
an imprint of Hodder Children's Books.

Commissioning Editor: Victoria Brooker   Book Editor: Katie Sergeant
Consultant: Carol Ballard   Picture Research: Katie Sergeant
Book Designer: Jane Hawkins   Cover: Hodder Children's Books

British Library Cataloguing in Publication Data
Woodward, Kay
  Taste. - (Our Senses)
  1.Taste - Juvenile literature
  I.Title
  612.8'7

ISBN 0750246723

Printed in China by WKT Company Ltd

Hodder Children's Books
A division of Hodder Headline Limited
338 Euston Road, London NW1 3BH

Cover: A girl eating an ice cream outdoors.

Picture Acknowledgements
The publisher would like to thank the following for permission to
reproduce their pictures: Corbis Imprint page and 17 (RNT
Productions), 10 (Richard Hutchings), 12 (Owen Franken), 16 (Danny
Lehman), 18 (Francine Fleischer), 19 (Royalty-Free), 20 (Richard
Cummins), 22 (right) (Royalty-Free); Getty Images
Cover (Stone/Cheryl Maeder), Title page and 11 (left) (Photodisc
Green/SW Productions/Royalty-Free), 4 (Stone/Paul Harris), 5
(Stone/Dave Nagel), 8 (Photodisc Green/SW Productions/Royalty-
Free), 9 (Photodisc Green/Buccina Studios/Royalty-Free), 13
(Stone/James Darell), 14 (Taxi/Greg Ceo), 15 (FoodPix/John E Kelly);
NHPA 21 (N A Callow); Wayland Picture Library 7, 11 (right), 22
(left), 23. Artwork on page 6 is by Peter Bull.

Contents

Words in **bold** can be found in the glossary on page 24.

Tastes everywhere!

The world is a tasty place. There are all sorts of food and drink to enjoy. Our **sense** of taste tells us what we like to eat and drink. This sense also tells us whether food is safe to eat.

▼ What fruit and vegetables do you like to taste?

▲ This boy is enjoying his ice cream!

You use your tongue to taste. You can taste food by licking it or by putting it in your mouth.

How we taste

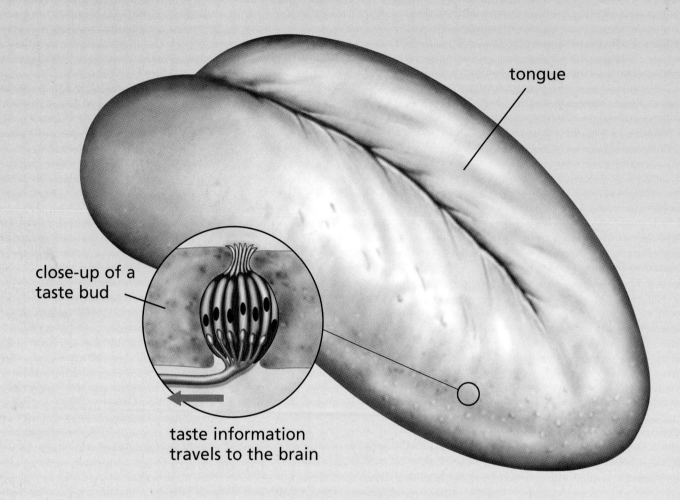

tongue

close-up of a taste bud

taste information travels to the brain

▲ There are thousands of taste buds all over your tongue.

Your tongue is covered with lots of tiny bumps called **taste buds**. When your tongue touches food, **information** about that food travels to your brain.

Your mouth makes a liquid called **saliva**. When food is too dry, your mouth makes more saliva. This makes it easier to taste and to eat.

Saliva helps you to swallow dry food like crackers. ▶

Flavour

Flavour is what something tastes like. Different types of food have different flavours. Strawberries, lemons, pizza and fish all have different flavours.

There are thousands of different
flavours in the food around us.
By mixing these flavours together,
people make tasty meals.

Sweet, salty, sour and bitter

The taste buds on your tongue can taste four main flavours. These flavours are sweet, salty, sour and bitter.

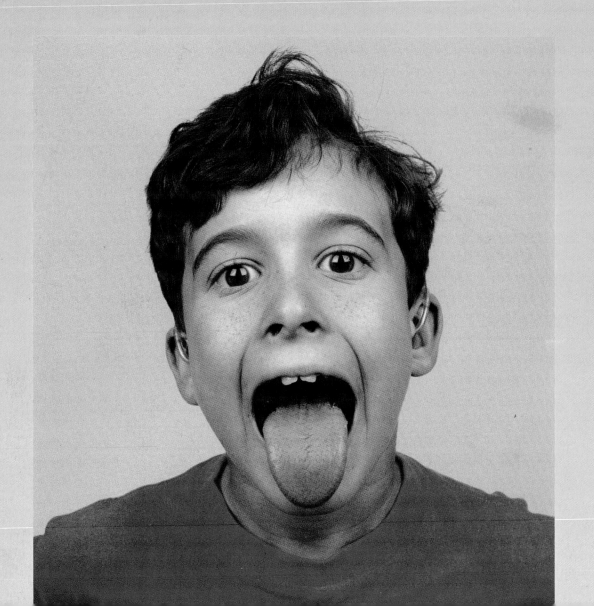

▼ Chocolate has a lovely sweet taste but lemons are sour.

Honey and chocolate are sweet. Savoury snacks and crisps are salty. Lemons and yoghurt are sour. Tonic water and banana skin are bitter.

Taste and smell

The senses of taste and smell are linked.
If you like the smell of a food or drink,
you will probably like the taste of it too.

With a cold and a blocked nose, it is difficult to smell and taste. As people grow older, they start to lose their senses of taste and smell.

Hot and cold

Some food tastes nicer when it is hot. Many people like to drink hot chocolate, coffee, tea and soup when the weather is cold. This makes them feel warmer.

Some food tastes nicer when it is cold. A chilled drink and cold salad are perfect for a hot day. A few types of food taste nice when they are hot or cold.

Around the world

Different flavours are popular in different countries around the world. In Italy, many people like to eat pizza and pasta. In Mexico, hot and spicy dishes are popular.

▲ You can eat food from around the world in your own home!

Today, more and more people travel around the world. They enjoy the food in **foreign** countries and then eat it when they are home.

Animals

Many animals can taste different things.
Dogs find it easy to taste sweet things.
Cats cannot taste sweet things at all.

Some undersea creatures do not taste with their tongues. Catfish have special whiskers that are covered with taste buds. Octopuses taste with the ends of their **tentacles**.

Minibeasts

Like humans, many minibeasts can taste food in their mouths. Some minibeasts can taste with other body parts. Blowflies and butterflies taste with their feet.

Honey bees taste with the tips of their **antennae**. They can check what food tastes like before they eat it.

Are you sweet, salty, sour or bitter?

1. Gather together different types of sweet, salty, sour and bitter food or drink. For example:

SWEET
Chocolate
Sugar

SALTY
Crisps
Salted nuts

SOUR
Lemons
Yoghurt

BITTER
Tonic water
Banana skin

2. Ask everyone to smell each type of food and drink. Did they like the smells?

3. Now ask everyone to taste each type of food and drink. Did they like the tastes?

You may find that when people liked the smell of something, they also liked the taste. This is because the senses of smell and taste are linked.

Now ask everyone which tastes they liked the best. Did everyone like the same things? Which tastes were most popular? Were any tastes unpopular?

Glossary

antennae	Long, thin body parts that stick out of an insect's head.
flavour	The taste of something.
foreign	Belonging to another country.
information	Things that tell you about something.
saliva	A liquid in your mouth that helps you to eat your food.
sense	The power to see, hear, smell, feel or taste.
taste buds	Tiny bumps on your tongue that taste things.
tentacle	A long bendy part of an octopus's body. An octopus has eight tentacles.

Index